from SEA TO SHINING SEA

CALIFORNIA

By Dennis Brindell Fradin

CONSULTANTS

Teena Stern, Archivist II, California State Archives, Sacramento

Robert L. Hillerich, Ph.D., Consultant, Pinellas County Schools, Florida;
Visiting Professor, University of South Florida

CHILDRENS PRESS®
CHICAGO

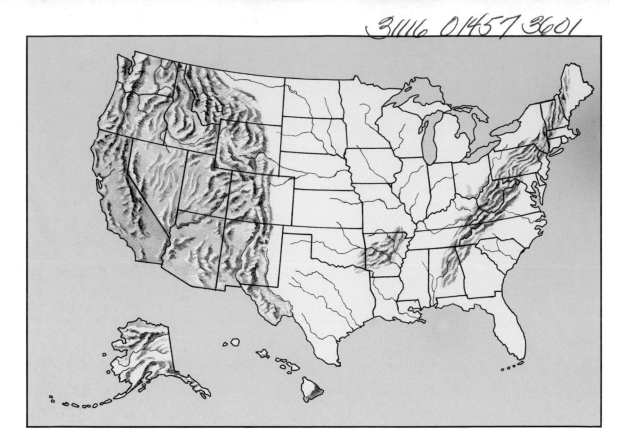

California is one of the three states in the region called the Pacific Coast. The other Pacific Coast states are Oregon and Washington.

For the Klingelhoffers—Bill, Jill, Sarah, Louis, and Jacob

Project Editor: Joan Downing
Design Director: Karen Kohn
Research Assistant: Judith Bloom Fradin
Typesetting: Graphic Connections, Inc.
Engraving: Liberty Photoengraving

SECOND PRINTING, 1993.

Library of Congress Cataloging-in-Publication Data

Fradin, Dennis B.
  California / by Dennis Brindell Fradin.
    p.   cm. — (From sea to shining sea)
  Includes index.
  Summary: An introduction to the "Golden State," our
most populated state and our top farming and
manufacturing state.
  ISBN 0-516-03805-2
  1. California—Juvenile literature. [1. California.]
I. Title. II. Series: Fradin, Dennis B. From sea to shining
sea.
F861.3.F718   1992   92-12944
976.8—dc20   CIP
                                            AC

Table of Contents

Costumed girls take part in a Japanese cherry blossom festival.

Introducing the Golden State

California is a state in the southwest corner of the country. An author in Spain coined the name *California* around 1510. He used the name for a magical, treasure-filled island. Later in the 1500s, Spanish explorers came to North America. They named California for the storybook island.

The real California proved to have treasures, too. In 1848, gold was discovered northeast of Sacramento. That caused the famous gold rush to California. California is now nicknamed the "Golden State." In 1892, another treasure was found. Oil was discovered in Los Angeles.

Today, California has the most people of the fifty states. It is the top farming and manufacturing state. California also has four of the country's fourteen largest cities. They are Los Angeles, San Diego, San Jose, and San Francisco.

California is special in many other ways. Where is the Golden Gate Bridge? Where are the world's tallest and oldest trees? Where is the nation's largest telescope? Where is Disneyland? The answer to these questions is: California!

A picture map
of California

Mountains, Deserts, and Redwood Trees

Mountains, Deserts, and Redwood Trees

California, Oregon, and Washington are called the Pacific Coast states. The Pacific Ocean splashes against western California. Oregon is California's neighbor to the north. Nevada and Arizona are to the east. The country of Mexico is to the south.

The Golden State is huge. Only Alaska and Texas are larger. Rhode Island, the smallest state, could fit inside California almost 130 times!

Death Valley (right) is the site of the lowest point in either North or South America.

TOPOGRAPHY

GEOGRAPHY

California has islands, mountains, valleys, and deserts. Its islands include Santa Catalina and the Channel Islands. Mountain ranges rise up along the ocean. Other mountains are farther inland. California's mountain peaks include Mount Whitney and Mount Shasta. Mount Whitney is in the Sierra Nevada. It stands 14,494 feet high. It is the country's tallest peak outside Alaska. Between California's coastal and inland mountains is the Great Valley. It's about 430 miles long.

The Golden State also has deserts. The Mojave Desert covers much of far southern California. Death Valley is another desert. It lies along California's border with Nevada. Part of Death Valley is 282 feet below sea level. This is the lowest point in either North or South America.

Farms nestle in one of California's many mountain valleys.

The Mojave Desert, near Barstow

Bristlecone pines like this one are the world's oldest trees.

Sea lions sun on the rocks near Monterey.

PLANTS AND ANIMALS

About 40 percent of California is wooded. California is home to the world's oldest trees. They are bristlecone pines. It is also home to the world's tallest trees, the redwoods. The world's most massive trees also grow in California. They are giant sequoias. Yucca trees and cactus plants are found in the deserts. The saguaro cactus can grow 60 feet high.

Many kinds of animals live in California. Whales and seals are found along the coast. Deer, bears, elk, foxes, bobcats, mountain lions, and coyotes live inland. The deserts are home to lizards and rattlesnakes. The California valley quail is the state bird. Eagles, falcons, ducks, and geese can also be spotted in California. San Juan Capistrano is known for its swallows. They arrive each year around March 19.

CLIMATE

California has a generally warm climate. Winter temperatures reach 60 degrees Fahrenheit in much of the state. Winters can be cold in the mountains, though. The state's all-time low temperature was

minus 45 degrees Fahrenheit. This occurred on January 20, 1937, in the Sierra Nevada in Boca.

Some mountain areas get hundreds of inches of snow each year. California holds the North American record for a monthly snowfall. In January 1911, 32.5 feet of snow fell at Tamarack. That was enough snow to cover a three-story building.

The ocean cools the coast in the summertime. July coastal temperatures often go above 70 degrees Fahrenheit. Summer desert temperatures often top 110 degrees Fahrenheit. On July 10, 1913, the temperature at Death Valley hit 134 degrees Fahrenheit. This is the record high temperature for all of North America.

A winter snowfall blankets the trees near El Capitan, a steep mountain in Yosemite National Park.

The highest temperature ever recorded on earth was 136 degrees Fahrenheit in Libya in 1922.

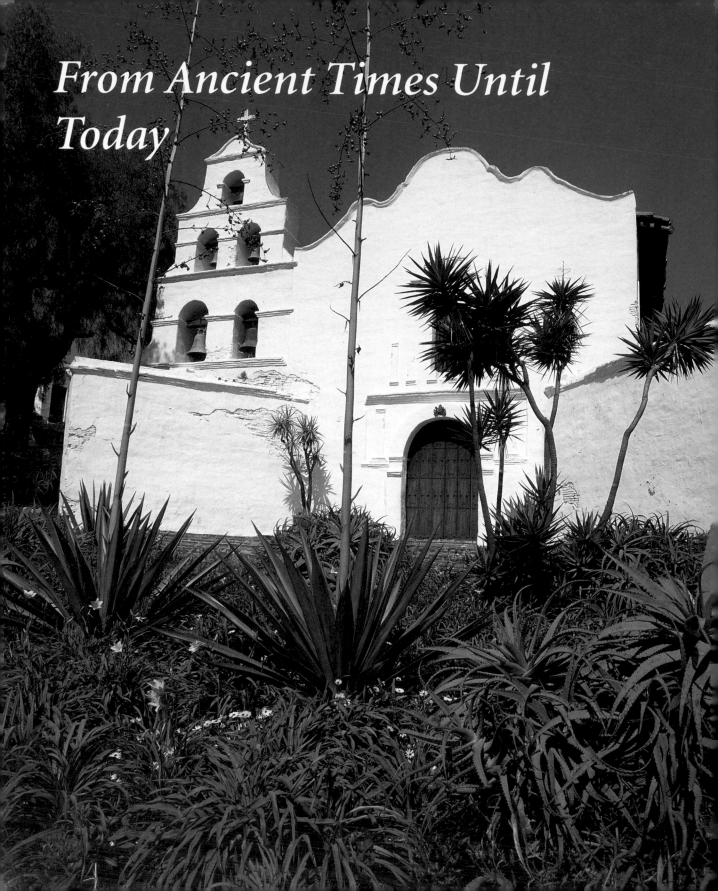

From Ancient Times Until Today

From Ancient Times Until Today

Millions of years ago, much of California lay under the ocean. Then, the ground quaked as mountains rose from the sea. Volcanoes formed in some mountains. Lava blew forth from the volcanoes. During the Ice Age, part of California was under glaciers.

Saber-toothed tigers lived in California long ago. They used their 8-inch-long teeth like swords. Mammoths and mastodons roamed about. Today's elephants are related to them. California was also home to dinosaurs. In 1936, a high-school student found dinosaur fossils near Modesto. This was the first dinosaur discovery on the West Coast.

The First Californians

People reached California at least 12,000 years ago. Early people drew pictures in California's caves and on cliffs. Many Native American groups lived in California in more recent times. They included the Hupa, Maidu, Miwok, Modoc, and Mojave. Still other groups were the Paiute, Shasta, and Yuma.

Early Californians made petroglyphs (rock carvings) at Lava Beds National Monument.

Feathered headdresses like these were worn by one group of early Californians.

Many of the Native Americans lived in wood and bark huts. The forest groups hunted deer. Coastal groups built redwood canoes and fished. Desert groups ate the fruits from saguaro cactuses and yucca trees. They made soap from yucca roots. They made baskets, rope, and sandals from the leaves. California's Native Americans made lovely baskets. Each group wove its own special design.

Explorers

Cabrillo was born in Portugal but worked for Spain.

Spaniards came to Mexico in 1519. Later, they explored lands to the north. Juan Rodríguez Cabrillo sailed from Mexico in 1542. He entered California's San Diego Bay that September. Cabrillo was the first known European to reach the

14

California coast. But Spain didn't settle California right away.

Sir Francis Drake of England reached California in 1579. He anchored his ship, the *Golden Hind*, near present-day San Francisco. Drake claimed California for England. But England did not act on this claim.

SPAIN RULES CALIFORNIA

More Spanish explorers reached California during the 1600s and 1700s. In 1769, Gaspar de Portolá led soldiers and priests from Mexico. Spanish priest Junipero Serra came with Portolá. In 1769, Father Serra founded a mission at San Diego. Portolá's soldiers built a *presidio* (fort) there that year. San Diego was California's first European settlement.

Father Serra founded eight more California missions besides that first one at San Diego.

More Spanish soldiers and priests arrived. By 1782, California had three more presidios. They were at Monterey, San Francisco, and Santa Barbara. A few Spanish families from Mexico also came to California. Yet, by 1820, only about 3,700 Spaniards lived there. By 1823, there were twenty-one missions along the California coast.

Thousands of Native Americans were brought to the missions. Often this was done against their will. They were taught Christianity. They grew the

The Russian chapel at Fort Ross State Historic Park

missions' crops. They also tended the cattle. Many of them died of disease.

Other people also moved to California. Russians arrived in 1812. They built Rossiya, north of San Francisco. This became known as Fort Ross. The Russians hunted sea otters along the coast. California's Russian River was named for them.

CALIFORNIA UNDER MEXICO

Mexico broke away from Spain in 1821. Mexico then took control of California. The Native Americans continued to live on mission lands. The mission lands were given mainly to people from Mexico. These people built ranches and farms on the old mission lands. Many of them grew very rich.

In the 1820s, American trappers and explorers entered California. The first American settlers arrived in 1841. Other Americans followed. They farmed and ranched. Some also opened businesses.

THE AMERICANS TAKE OVER

Many of the Americans wanted California to join the United States. In 1846, the United States and

Mexico went to war. This is known as the Mexican War (1846-1848). It was fought over California, Texas, and other matters.

On June 14, 1846, Americans seized Sonoma. This is near San Francisco. The rebels proclaimed that California was free of Mexico. They called the region the California Republic. The rebels made a flag. It had a star, a grizzly bear, and the words *California Republic*. This flag is now the state's flag.

John Charles Frémont, Stephen Watts Kearny, and Robert Stockton led the American troops. They seized one California town after another. The Americans won the Mexican War in 1848. California became part of the United States that year. But California was not yet a state.

THE GOLD RUSH

On January 24, 1848, James Marshall was building a sawmill for John Sutter on the American River. Suddenly, Marshall spotted something shiny. It was gold!

The news spread. Soon thousands of people headed for California. They came by wagon and ship. Most of them arrived in 1849. That's why these miners were called forty-niners.

In 1846, Americans raised the Bear Flag and proclaimed that California was free of Mexico.

In 1848, gold was discovered at Sutter's Mill (below).

Forty-niners washing gold in the Sierra Nevada during the California gold rush

Levi Strauss reached San Francisco from New York City in 1850.

The miners built mining camps and towns. Some people struck it rich. But most found little gold. They had trouble paying their bills. Goods were very costly. Two eggs could cost six dollars.

Instead of mining, many people opened businesses. Levi Strauss began making heavy work pants for miners. The miners called the pants "Levis." Millions of people wear Levis today.

The great gold rush changed California forever. When Marshall discovered gold, only about 15,000 people other than Native Americans lived in California. San Francisco had only a few hundred people. Sacramento didn't even exist. About 90,000 people came to California in 1849. That year, Sacramento was founded. It was not far from the gold discovery. San Francisco grew into a big supply center for the miners.

On September 9, 1850, California became the thirty-first state. Since 1854, Sacramento has been California's capital.

THE YOUNG STATE

The gold rush ended about 1855. But people still poured into California. Between 1850 and 1860, California gained more than 280,000 people. They included Chinese, Irish, Germans, Italians, and people from many other countries.

Californians had one big complaint. They were cut off from most of the country. It took weeks for letters from the East Coast to arrive. They came by stagecoach. It took two months for news of California's statehood to reach San Francisco.

Things improved in 1860. The Pony Express opened. Relay teams of riders carried mail between Missouri and California. Mail was delivered in a few days. The telegraph reached California in 1861. Californians could then quickly contact the East. In 1869, a railroad also linked California and the East.

From 1860 to 1861, Pony Express riders carried mail between Missouri and California.

Los Angeles is called L.A. for short.

Workers help clear the wreckage after the 1906 San Francisco earthquake and fire.

Railroads soon helped Los Angeles grow into a big city. By 1890, L.A. had more than 50,000 people. In 1892, oil was found there. Soon, oil was being pumped from hundreds of wells. California was the top oil-producing state by 1900.

EARTHQUAKES, AQUEDUCTS, AND MOVIES

California often has small earthquakes. Now and then it is rocked by a big quake. One occurred on April 18, 1906. At 5:12 that morning, buildings began toppling. The quake lasted a little over a minute. But it set off fires that raged for three days. About 700 people died in the Great San Francisco Earthquake and Fire. About 300,000 people lost their homes.

San Francisco was rebuilt with earthquake safety in mind. Other California cities also passed laws to protect buildings from earthquakes. The state has been shaken by big quakes for many years. In October 1989, a quake hit the San Francisco Bay area. It killed sixty-seven people. The safety laws kept the number of deaths low.

Los Angeles also had a problem in the early 1900s. The city needed more water. The Los Angeles Aqueduct was completed in 1913. This

233-mile canal carries water to L.A. The water comes from rivers in the Sierra Nevada. Many other canals have been built. Their water has made southern California a great farming area.

A new industry came to L.A. in the early 1900s. This was moviemaking. L.A.'s Hollywood section became the moviemaking center of the world. Hollywood movies have entertained billions of people. They have also helped Americans get through hard times.

San Francisco as it looked after the earthquake and fire

The movie companies liked California's warm weather and varied scenery.

World Wars, Depression, and Growth

Americans suffered rough times in the early and mid-1900s. The United States entered World War I (1914-1918) in 1917. About 20,000 Californians helped win this war.

The Great Depression hit America in 1929. Banks and factories closed. Farmers lost their land. This occurred in every state. But California had an added problem. Between 1934 and 1940, 365,000 people moved to California. They were seeking a

Airplanes for use in World War II were made at the Douglas Aircraft plant in Santa Monica.

better life. Many of these people couldn't find work in California. They had to live in shacks, in their cars, in tents, or wherever they could.

With the coming of World War II (1939-1945), people found jobs. On December 7, 1941, Japan bombed Pearl Harbor. Then, the United States entered the war. About 750,000 Californians served in this war. Californians at home also helped. They built airplanes, ships, and weapons.

Many Japanese Americans lived in California. The government feared that they would side with Japan. About 110,000 Japanese Americans were rounded up. Most of them were from California. Others were from Washington and Oregon. These people were forced into special camps. But there was no reason to doubt their loyalty. Many Japanese Americans fought for the United States.

In April 1945, delegates from fifty countries met in San Francisco. They organized the United Nations (UN). This body works for world peace.

After World War II, people's interest in outer space grew. In 1947, America's largest telescope was completed. It's at Palomar Observatory near San Diego. Astronomers have used it to unlock many secrets of the universe. The Jet Propulsion Laboratory is in Pasadena. In 1958, it became part

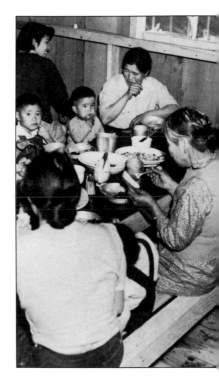

Japanese Americans from California were forced to live in internment camps during World War II.

of the United States space program. The lab guided *Surveyor I*. It landed on the moon in 1966.

California continued to grow during these years. In 1963, it passed New York State for having the most people. The state continues to grow. The 1990 census counted 29,760,021 Californians. But with this growth have come big problems.

CURRENT PROBLEMS

Poverty is a big problem in California. One-fourth of all California children are poor. Many of their parents cannot find jobs. By 1992, the state had one of the country's highest jobless rates.

California has thousands of migrant workers. These workers are mostly Mexicans. They move from farm to farm harvesting crops. They have jobs. Yet, they are very poor. They are paid little.

Pollution is another big problem. Some California cities suffer from smog. This air pollution comes from car and factory fumes. Oil spills and other wastes have sometimes spoiled parts of California's shoreline. Other chemicals have leaked into the ground. They have harmed the drinking water in places.

People and pollution have wiped out many

kinds of animals. The California grizzly bear became extinct in 1922. Today, it is seen only on the state flag. The California desert tortoise and the spotted owl are now in danger.

California faces serious water shortages. This happens even when there is rain. A major drought hit California in the late 1980s. It lasted into the 1990s. Water supplies dried up due to the lack of rain. People are asked to use less water.

In 1991, shocked Americans saw a videotape on TV. It showed four white L.A. policemen beating a black motorist. In 1992, the policemen were found not guilty of using excessive force. The verdict sparked huge riots in South Central L.A. More than 40 people died and nearly 4,000 fires were set.

Californians are trying to solve their problems. They hope to see results by the year 2000. That will be California's 150th birthday as a state.

Left: Workers clean up Huntington Beach after a 1990 oil spill. Right: A migrant worker pushes a wheelbarrow full of grapes he has picked.

Californians and Their Work

CALIFORNIANS AND THEIR WORK

Its 29,760,021 people make California the biggest state. California has the most white, Hispanic, and Asian people. It has the second-largest number of blacks and Native Americans. California also is one of the country's fastest-growing states. Each day, California grows by about 2,000 people.

Four of the country's fourteen largest cities are in California. Los Angeles is the second-biggest United States city. Only New York City is bigger. San Diego places sixth. San Jose ranks eleventh. San Francisco is in fourteenth place.

More Asian and Hispanic people live in California than in any other state.

CALIFORNIANS AT WORK

California is the top manufacturing and farming state. It is also a leading mining and fishing state. If it were a country, California would be about the eighth richest.

About 2.2 million Californians make products. California leads the country at making airplanes. Californians also make cars, spacecraft, boats, motorcycles, and bicycles. They also lead at making

Telephone company workers

A park ranger at Sequoia National Park

computers, foods, and medical instruments. The state is near the top at making musical instruments and art supplies. Jewelry, toys, sporting goods, clothing, books, paints, and silverware are other important products. California is also a leader in refining oil.

About 3 million Californians sell goods. Another 3.3 million provide other services.

Service workers include many people in the tourist business. California is a leading vacation state.

California has about 2 million government workers. This is more than any other state. Government workers range from teachers to soldiers. The state has several major military posts. Among them is the San Diego Naval Base. Nearby is Camp Pendleton, a Marine base.

About 400,000 Californians work at farming. The state is a major producer of milk and eggs. Beef cattle, sheep, and turkeys are also leading farm goods. California grows half the country's fruits and vegetables. It leads in grapes, strawberries, lettuce, and tomatoes. Cotton, oranges, walnuts, and broccoli are other important crops.

About 50,000 Californians work at mining. California ranks third at producing oil. Oil is the state's top mining product. The Golden State ranks second at mining gold. Only Nevada mines more. California is a leading producer of natural gas. The state mines the most sand and gravel and tungsten. Boron is mined only in California.

Many Californians make a living by fishing. California leads the country at catching tuna. Other fish are salmon, swordfish, and herring. California shellfish include shrimp and crabs.

Tungsten is used in high-speed tools, electric lights, and television sets. Boron goes into soaps and medicines.

Californians work in many different fields, including electronics (left) and flower farming (right).

A Trip Through the Golden State

A Trip Through the Golden State

California has plenty to attract visitors. Its seacoast is popular with swimmers and surfers. The redwood forests and Yosemite National Park draw nature lovers. Skiing is popular in the mountains. It has exciting cities. Disneyland is a favorite place for families to visit.

Each year, forty million people from out of state visit California. This is more people than live in the state.

The Southern Coast

San Diego is in the state's southwest corner. It is a good place to start a trip up the coast. San Diego is called the "Birthplace of California." A cross marks the spot where Spaniards first settled California in 1769. Nearby is the Junipero Serra Museum. There, visitors can learn about San Diego's early days.

San Diego has a wonderful climate. This has helped make it one of America's fastest-growing cities. Los Angeles is the only California city that is larger. About a fifth of all San Diegans are Hispanic. Most of these people have roots in Mexico. Mexican foods, music, and festivals are popular in San Diego. San Diego is just north of Mexico. From San Diego, many people take trips to Tijuana, Mexico.

Building sand castles at a San Diego beach

The San Diego Zoo is one of the city's attractions. It has 800 different kinds of animals. San Diego's Sea World has dolphins and other sea animals. Sports fans enjoy the city's pro teams. The Padres play baseball. The football team is the Chargers.

Visitors pet the sea animals at San Diego's Sea World.

Palomar Observatory is northeast of San Diego. There, visitors can see the country's biggest telescope. This is the Hale telescope. Its mirror is 200 inches across.

Palomar Observatory

California's biggest city is north of San Diego. This is Los Angeles. It was founded as a Spanish town in 1781. Today, L.A. has almost 3.5 million people. About half of the fifty states have fewer people than that! L.A. is huge in area, too. The city covers 464 square miles. It is nearly half as big as the state of Rhode Island.

The city's people are called Angelenos. Many of the families came from all parts of the world.

Some movies and television shows are made in Los Angeles. Several movie studios offer tours.

Los Angeles also has many pro sports teams. The Dodgers play baseball, and the Rams and Raiders play football. The Kings play hockey. L.A.'s basketball teams are the Lakers and the Clippers.

Left: An animator working at a Hollywood studio in Los Angeles Right: The castle at Disneyland, in Anaheim

34

La Brea tar pits are also in L.A. Long ago, animals came to drink water at the pits. Many of them got caught in the tar and died. Skeletons of saber-toothed tigers, camels, and mammoths have been found there. Visitors can view these skeletons at the Page Museum of La Brea Discoveries. It's near the tar pits.

A display at La Brea tar pits

Just southeast of L.A. is Anaheim. Disneyland is there. Walt Disney opened this amusement park in 1955. Each year, Disneyland is visited by about ten million people. Pro sports fans also visit Anaheim. The L.A. Rams play football there. The California Angels play baseball.

Just north of L.A. is Pasadena. Each New Year's Day a famous college football game is played there. It is called the Rose Bowl. The Tournament of Roses Parade is held that morning.

The Santa Barbara mission

Santa Barbara is north of Los Angeles. Santa Barbara is an old mission town. It was founded in 1786. The city is full of Spanish-style buildings. They are made of white stucco. Red tiles cover the roofs. The Channel Islands are off Santa Barbara. These islands are a good place to see whales, seals, and dolphins.

Many people dream of living in a castle. Newspaper publisher William Randolph Hearst did

Big Sur

that. His home was Hearst Castle. It is north of Santa Barbara at San Simeon. Visitors can see great artworks that Hearst collected.

North of San Simeon is Big Sur. This is a rugged 100-mile stretch of coast. It has some of America's most scenic cliffs and beaches. Big Sur extends to Carmel. Many authors and artists have lived in this little town. Father Junipero Serra died at the mission he founded there. He is buried at the mission.

THE SAN FRANCISCO BAY REGION

San Francisco Bay is north of Carmel. Three major cities lie around the bay. They are San Jose, San Francisco, and Oakland.

San Jose is just south of the bay. It was founded in 1777 as California's first *pueblo* (city). For many years, San Jose was mainly a farming center. Now, computers, spacecraft, and missiles are made there. These industries have brought more people to the city. Today, San Jose is the state's third-largest city.

The Rosicrucian Egyptian Museum is a highlight of San Jose. Mummies and other objects from ancient Egypt are displayed there. Pro hockey fans watch the San Jose Sharks.

San Francisco is one of the world's prettiest cities. It lies on the bay. Spaniards founded San Francisco in 1776. Today, San Francisco is the state's fourth-biggest city.

San Francisco is hilly. In 1873, Andrew Hallidie invented cable cars. They make traveling up and down San Francisco's hills easy. Besides, they're fun to ride. The Golden Gate Bridge adds to San Francisco's beauty. It stands at the entrance of San Francisco Bay. People travel north and south on it.

One-third of all San Franciscans have Asian backgrounds, including Chinese, Japanese, Vietnamese, and others. San Francisco's Chinatown

Left: One of San Francisco's famous cable cars
Right: The San Francisco-Oakland Bay Bridge and a moonlit view of San Francisco

37

is home to 30,000 people of Chinese background. It is one of North America's largest Chinese neighborhoods. The Asian Art Museum and the Japanese Tea Garden are in Golden Gate Park.

Fisherman's Wharf is another highlight of San Francisco. Its markets sell fresh seafood. Shoppers there can also buy tasty sourdough bread.

San Franciscans follow two pro sports teams. The Giants play baseball. The 49ers play football. Both teams use famous Candlestick Park.

Oakland is just across the bay. The San Francisco-Oakland Bay Bridge links the two cities. Oakland was founded in 1850. Today, Oakland is California's sixth-largest city. Oakland has had to

Fresh seafood tempts strollers and shoppers at San Francisco's Fisherman's Wharf.

recover from two recent disasters. A 1989 earthquake caused $6 billion in damages. In 1991, a big fire killed 25 people. It destroyed about 3,500 houses and apartments.

The Oakland Museum is a good place to learn about California. The museum's redwood forest is a favorite with children. The exhibit on the gold rush is also enjoyable.

Oakland also has two pro sports teams. The Athletics (A's) play baseball. The Golden State Warriors play basketball.

The Oakland A's

North of Oakland lie the Sonoma and Napa valleys. They are covered with grapevines. The grapes are used to make wine.

THE NORTHERN COAST

Point Reyes National Seashore

The California coast does not have any big cities north of San Francisco Bay. But there are many places of great beauty. Point Reyes National Seashore is such a place. It is north of San Francisco. People explore rocky cliffs and beaches there.

The Redwood Highway follows along California's northern coast. The highway passes through Eureka. This city is in northwest California. Eureka has long been a logging center. The Carson

The William Carson Mansion, in Eureka

Mount Shasta stands 14,162 feet high.

Mansion is in Eureka. Lumberman William Carson built this eighteen-room home in 1886. Much of it is made of redwood.

The Redwood Highway goes through redwood groves. They include those at Redwood National Park in northwest California. Many of the park's redwoods are over 200 feet tall. A 368-foot redwood there is the world's tallest tree.

THE NORTHERN INTERIOR

California's northern interior is known for its woods and mountains. This is a great area for hiking. Shasta-Trinity National Forest alone has 1,300 miles of hiking trails. Mount Shasta is in the forest. Long ago, volcanoes blasted lava from Mount Shasta. Today, skiers come down its slopes.

Lava Beds National Monument is in northeastern California. Millions of years ago, lava poured out of a volcano there. Over time, the hot bubbling lava hardened. Volcanic cones and caves were formed. They can be seen at the monument.

South of the lava beds is Lassen Peak. It is the most recent volcano to erupt in California. Lassen Peak was last active in 1921. It is in Lassen Volcanic National Park.

South of Lassen Peak is Sacramento. This is northern California's biggest inland city. Gold was found at John Sutter's sawmill to the northeast in 1848. His son, John Sutter, Jr., founded Sacramento the next year. Sacramento has been California's capital since 1854. State lawmakers meet at the state capitol. The small dome atop the state capitol contains California gold.

Sacramento has other places to visit. Sutter's Fort has displays about John Sutter's life. The California State Railroad Museum is America's largest railroad museum. The State Indian Museum has displays about California's Native Americans.

Left: California redwood trees
Right: The state capitol, at Sacramento

41

Lake Tahoe

Baskets, dugout canoes, and weapons can be seen. Sports fans can watch the Sacramento Kings. That is the city's pro basketball team.

East of Sacramento is Lake Tahoe. It is on the elbow-shaped bend at the California-Nevada border. This is a popular vacation spot. Lake Tahoe goes down to a depth of 1,685 feet. It is one of America's deepest lakes.

THE CENTRAL INTERIOR

Yosemite National Park is 75 miles south of Lake Tahoe. This park is known for its mountains, lakes, and waterfalls. Yosemite Falls is the country's highest waterfall. It has a total drop of 2,425 feet. That's nearly half a mile. Ribbon Falls is the country's second-highest waterfall. It is also in the park.

East of Yosemite are the White Mountains. Methuselah, a bristlecone pine tree, grows there. Methuselah is over 4,600 years old.

West of Yosemite is Angels Camp. Every year the town hosts a special event. This is the frog-jumping contest of Calaveras County. A story by Mark Twain started this contest. The story was called "The Celebrated Jumping Frog of Calaveras County."

The Calaveras County frog-jumping contest is an annual event.

South of Angels Camp is Fresno. It is near California's exact center. During the 1980s, Fresno was America's fastest-growing big city.

Fresno is in the San Joaquin Valley. This is a big farming region. Fresno County has about 8,000 farms. That's more than any other American county. Fresno County leads the country in growing grapes, cotton, and tomatoes. Farm products are packed and shipped in Fresno.

The Fresno region produces most of the nation's raisins, which are made from grapes.

Kings Canyon and Sequoia national parks are east of Fresno. These two parks are run as one. The parks' snow-capped peaks include Mount Whitney.

Upper Yosemite Falls

The General Sherman sequoia is the largest tree on earth.

A trail leads to the top. The parks are also home to giant sequoias. They are the world's biggest trees. One of these giants is the General Sherman Tree. It is the largest tree on earth. The General Sherman is 275 feet tall. Its trunk is 103 feet around. This trunk weighs three million pounds. That's as much as 300 large elephants!

Death Valley is east of the parks. It's at the Nevada border. This desert is in Death Valley National Monument. Only about 2 inches of rain fall there each year. Despite its name, Death Valley is far from lifeless. Bobcats, coyotes, and foxes live there. Visitors also spot rabbits, lizards, and bighorn sheep. Birds called roadrunners race about. Cactuses and bristlecone pines are among the plant life.

THE SOUTHERN INTERIOR

California's southern interior is another big farming area. San Bernardino County is a big milk producer. It has the most milk cows of any American county. Imperial County grows the most hay. Riverside County is a top egg producer.

The Bakersfield region is a huge oil-producing area. In nearby Taft is the West Kern Oil Museum. Displays show how oil is formed, mined, and used.

Joshua Tree National Monument is southeast of Taft. Groves of Joshua trees grow there. They are a kind of yucca tree.

South of the Joshua trees is the Salton Sea. It's a good place to end a California trip. The Salton Sea is really a shallow, salty lake. From 1905 to 1907, the Colorado River flooded this low-lying area. The water mixed with ground salt. This formed the Salton Sea. Today, people boat and fish there.

Salton Sea National Wildlife Refuge is at the lake. It has hundreds of kinds of birds. Pelicans and peregrine falcons nest there. These falcons are the fastest-flying birds in the world. They can reach speeds of 220 miles per hour.

Left: A Joshua tree at the Joshua Tree National Monument Right: A girl making tracks in the sand dunes at Death Valley National Monument

45

A Gallery
of
Famous
Californians

A Gallery of Famous Californians

California has produced many famous people. They include Native American leaders, movie stars, and presidents. Well-known writers and athletes also call California home.

Junipero Serra (1713-1784) was born in Spain. For many years, he taught college on Majorca. In 1749, he sailed to the New World. Father Serra founded nine missions in California.

Captain Jack (1837-1873) was born at the California-Oregon border. He was a Modoc originally called **Kintpuash.** The U.S. government began to push the Modocs off their land. They fought back in the Modoc War (1872-1873). Captain Jack led them. About fifty warriors hid in California's lava beds. For months they held off nearly 1,000 U.S. troops. Finally, the army shelled the Modocs out of the lava beds. Captain Jack was hanged. His people were sent to a reservation in Oklahoma.

Luther Burbank (1849-1926) moved to California as a young man. Burbank created the Shasta daisy. He developed the plumcot. It's a mixture of the plum and apricot.

Father Junipero Serra

Luther Burbank

Left: Dianne Feinstein
Right: Ronald and
Nancy Reagan

George Smith Patton, Jr. (1885-1945) was born in San Gabriel. He became an army general. Known for his toughness, Patton was called "Old Blood and Guts." He led tanks in Europe during World War II.

Richard Nixon was born in 1913 in Yorba Linda. He graduated from California's Whittier College. In 1946, Nixon was elected to the U.S. Congress. Later, he was the country's vice-president (1953-1961). In 1969, he became president. Nixon took the country out of the Vietnam War. He also improved U.S. relations with Russia and China. Nixon quit as president in 1974. He had covered up crimes of his political workers. This is called the Watergate scandal.

Ronald Reagan was born in Illinois in 1911. Later, he became a Hollywood movie actor. Reagan was elected governor of California in 1966. In 1981, he became president of the United States.

Thomas Bradley was born in Texas in 1917. He later moved to Los Angeles. There, he worked as a policeman and as a lawyer. In 1973, Bradley became the city's first black mayor. By 1992, Bradley had been L.A.'s mayor for nearly twenty years.

Dianne Feinstein was born in San Francisco in 1933. She was San Francisco's mayor from 1978 to 1988. Feinstein made many changes in downtown San Francisco.

Cesar Chavez was born in Arizona in 1927. When he was a child, his family lost their farm. They became migrant farm workers in California. Later, Chavez helped found a farm workers' union. It is the United Farm Workers of America.

Ansel Adams (1902-1984) was born in San Francisco. He became a great photographer. His best-known pictures are of Yosemite National Park.

Isadora Duncan (1878-1927) was also born in San Francisco. She helped create modern dance.

General George Patton

Isadora Duncan

Many great movie stars were born in the Golden State. **Shirley Temple** was the most famous child star of all time. She was born in Santa Monica in 1928. Two of her films were *The Little Colonel* and *Captain January*. **Cher** was born in El Centro in 1946. She won an Academy Award for best actress in 1988 for her role in *Moonstruck*.

One of California's most famous film stars isn't a person. His name is **Mickey Mouse**. Walt Disney created Mickey in a Los Angeles studio in 1928. The first Mickey Mouse cartoon was *Steamboat Willie*. It came out in 1928. Mickey still looks much the same as he did then.

California has also produced many great athletes. **James Corbett** (1866-1933) was born in San Francisco. "Gentleman Jim" became a pro boxer. He held the heavyweight crown from 1892 to 1897.

Billie Jean King was born in Long Beach in 1943. She became a great tennis star. **O. J.**

Left: James Corbett, who was called "Gentleman Jim" because of his good manners and his fancy clothes
Right: Tennis star Billie Jean King

Simpson was born in San Francisco in 1947. He led in pro football rushing four times.

Swimmer **Mark Spitz** was born in Modesto in 1950. Spitz won seven gold medals in the 1972 Summer Olympics. No American has won more gold medals at one Olympics. **Kristi Yamaguchi** was born in Fremont in 1971. Yamaguchi was ice skating by the time she was six. In 1992, she won an Olympic gold medal for figure skating.

Two pitchers in baseball's Hall of Fame are Californians. **Don Drysdale** was born in Van Nuys in 1936. He pitched six straight shutouts in 1968. **Tom Seaver** was born in Fresno in 1944. He once struck out ten straight batters.

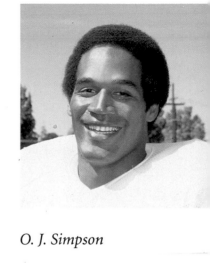

O. J. Simpson

Kristi Yamaguchi

Ted Williams

Jack London

Two big hitters in baseball's Hall of Fame are also Californians. **Joe DiMaggio** was born in Martinez in 1914. In 1941, he got a hit in fifty-six straight games. No one has come close to this record. **Ted Williams** was born in San Diego in 1918. In six different years, he had the best batting average. In 1941, he hit a record .406. The state that grows the most strawberries also produced **Darryl Strawberry**. He was born in L.A. in 1962. Strawberry is one of the best home-run hitters today.

John Steinbeck (1902-1968) was a great California writer. He was born in Salinas. His best-known novel is *The Grapes of Wrath*. It is about a poor farm family that moves to California. Steinbeck won a Pulitzer Prize for that book in 1940. Author **Jack London** (1876-1916) was born in San Francisco. He wrote *The Call of the Wild* and *White Fang*. They are novels about dogs. **Arnold Lobel** (1933-1987) was an author and artist of children's books. He was born in L.A. Lobel won the 1981 Caldecott Medal for his artwork in *Fables*. His other books include *Frog and Toad Are Friends* and *Mouse Tales*.

Sally Ride went far in the world. She actually left the earth. Ride was born in Encino in 1951. She

Astronaut Sally Ride was the first U. S. woman in space.

became an astronaut. In 1983, she flew on the space shuttle *Challenger*. Ride became the first U.S. woman in space.

Home to Sally Ride, Joe DiMaggio, Captain Jack, Luther Burbank, and Shirley Temple . . .

Home also to the world's oldest, tallest, and biggest trees . . .

The site of Disneyland, Yosemite National Park, Death Valley, and Hollywood . . .

The state that has the most people, and that is number one in farming and manufacturing . . .

This is California, the Golden State!

Did You Know?

Lombard Street is in San Francisco. It is the steepest and most crooked street in the United States.

There are 195 United States cities with over 100,000 people. California alone has forty-three of them.

Edgar Rice Burroughs, author of the Tarzan books, lived in California. The L.A. suburb of Tarzana was named for Burroughs' famous hero.

There are more than one hundred chemical elements, such as oxygen, helium, gold, and silver. Californium is the only element named for a state. It was discovered at the University of California at Berkeley in 1950.

California has some tasty place names. The Chocolate Mountains are in California. So are the towns of Apple Valley, Cherry Valley, Lemon Grove, Honeydew, Orange, Peanut, Pumpkin Center, Raisin, Rice, and Strawberry.

The world's largest map is kept at Hamilton Air Force Base in Novato, California. This map of California is 45 feet by 18 feet. It weighs about 86,000 pounds.

Shirley Temple was the most popular movie star in the world in 1937. For her ninth birthday that year, her fans sent Shirley 135,000 gifts. They included hundreds of dolls and a live baby kangaroo.

A fault is an ancient break in the earth's crust. Plates of bedrock come together at a fault line. When they shift, an earthquake occurs. The San Andreas Fault is the most dangerous fault line in California. It stretches from the northern California coast to the Mexican border.

Other California towns with unusual names include Cool, Fallen Leaf, Rainbow, Volcano, and Weed Patch.

55

California Information

State flag

Golden poppies

Area: 158,693 square miles (the third-largest state)

Greatest Distance North to South: 646 miles

Greatest Distance East to West: 560 miles

Borders: Oregon to the north; Nevada and Arizona to the east; Mexico to the south; the Pacific Ocean to the west

Highest Point: Mount Whitney, 14,494 feet above sea level

Lowest Point: 282 feet below sea level, in Death Valley

Hottest Recorded Temperature: 134° F. (in Death Valley, on July 10, 1913)

Coldest Recorded Temperature: -45° F. (in Boca in the Sierra Nevada, on January 20, 1937)

Statehood: The thirty-first state, on September 9, 1850

Origin of Name: *California* was the name of a treasure-filled island in a Spanish story of the early 1500s

Capital: Sacramento (since 1854)

Counties: 58

United States Representatives: 52 (as of 1992)

State Senators: 40

State Assembly Members: 80

State Song: "I Love You, California," by F. B. Silverwood (words) and A. F. Frankenstein (music)

State Motto: *Eureka* (Greek for "I have found it")

Nickname: The Golden State

State Seal: Adopted in 1849

State Flag: Adopted in 1911

State Flower: Golden poppy

State Bird: California valley quail

State Insect: California dog-face butterfly

State Fish: Golden trout

State Mineral: Gold

State Tree: California redwood

State Animal: California grizzly bear

State Marine Mammal: California gray whale

State Fossil: Saber-toothed tiger

Some Rivers: Sacramento, San Joaquin, Colorado, American, Feather, Klamath, Trinity, Russian

Some Mountain Ranges: Sierra Nevada, Cascade, Klamath, Panamint, San Bernardino

Main Deserts: Mojave, Colorado, Death Valley

Some Wildlife: Whales, seals, deer, bears, elk, foxes, bobcats, mountain lions, coyotes, lizards, rattlesnakes, bighorn sheep, desert tortoises, California valley quails, eagles, ducks, geese, roadrunners, swallows, many other kinds of birds

Some Manufactured Products: Airplanes, spacecraft, and other transportation equipment, computers and other kinds of electronics, foods, wines, medical instruments, musical instruments, jewelry, toys, sporting goods, clothing, furniture, paper, books, soap, paint, silverware, refined oil

Some Farm Products: Milk, beef cattle, horses, turkeys, chickens, sheep, cotton, rice, eggs, grapes, strawberries, oranges, lemons, almonds, lettuce, watermelons, sugar beets, plums, carrots, tomatoes, avocados, other fruits and vegetables

Some Mining Products: Oil, sand and gravel, natural gas, gold, boron, tungsten, gypsum

Some Fishing Products: Tuna, salmon, herring, swordfish, shrimp, crabs

Population: 29,760,021, the most populous state (1990 U.S. Census Bureau figures)

Major Cities (1990 U.S. Census):

Los Angeles	3,485,398	Oakland	372,242
San Diego	1,110,549	Sacramento	369,365
San Jose	782,248	Fresno	354,202
San Francisco	723,959	Santa Ana	293,742
Long Beach	429,433	Anaheim	266,406

Redwood tree

California valley quail

California History

10,000 B.C.—Early people are living in California

1542—Juan Rodríguez Cabrillo explores California's coast for Spain

1579—Sir Francis Drake of England explores California

1769—Spaniards Gaspar de Portolá and Father Junipero Serra found San Diego, California's first European settlement

1776—San Francisco is founded

1781—Los Angeles is founded

1812—Russians build Rossiya (Fort Ross)

1821—Mexico frees itself from Spain

1822—Mexico takes control of California

1834—The mission system is taken away from the Catholic church

1841—The first big wagon train of Americans reaches California

1846—Americans seize Sonoma in the Bear Flag Revolt and proclaim the California Republic

1848—The Americans win the Mexican War; California becomes part of the United States; James Marshall discovers gold at Sutter's mill

1849—The forty-niners come to California in the gold rush

1850—On September 9, California becomes the thirty-first state

1854—Sacramento becomes the permanent state capital

1860—The Pony Express links California to the East

1861—The telegraph reaches California

1869—The railroad connects California to the East

1892—Oil is found in Los Angeles

1905-07—Flooding from the Colorado River creates the Salton Sea

1906—About 700 people die in the Great San Francisco Earthquake and Fire

During Living History Days at Sutter's Fort State Historic Park in Sacramento, visitors find out how early Californians lived.

1913—The Los Angeles Aqueduct is completed

1917-18—After the United States enters World War I, 20,000 Californians serve

1929-39—During the Great Depression, about 365,000 people move to California

1933—About 120 people die in the Long Beach earthquake

1941-45—After the United States enters World War II, 750,000 Californians serve

1945—The United Nations is organized in San Francisco

1947—A giant telescope at Palomar Observatory is completed

1953—California governor Earl Warren becomes chief justice of the United States Supreme Court

1955—Disneyland opens in Anaheim

1963—California becomes the most populous state

1969—Richard Nixon of California becomes the thirty-seventh president of the United States

1971—An earthquake in the Los Angeles area kills about sixty-five people

1981—Ronald Reagan becomes the fortieth president of the United States

1989—An earthquake in the San Francisco Bay area kills sixty-seven people and causes $6 billion in damages

1990—California's population reaches 29,760,021

1991—An Oakland fire kills 25 people and destroys about 3,500 homes and apartments; an amateur videotape of four white L.A. policemen beating black motorist Rodney King stuns the nation

1992—More than 40 people die and most of South Central L.A is destroyed by fire when riots erupt after the acquittal of policemen in the Rodney King case; two earthquakes, one the strongest in 40 years, shake southern California

Richard Nixon was president of the United States from 1969 to 1974.

MAP KEY

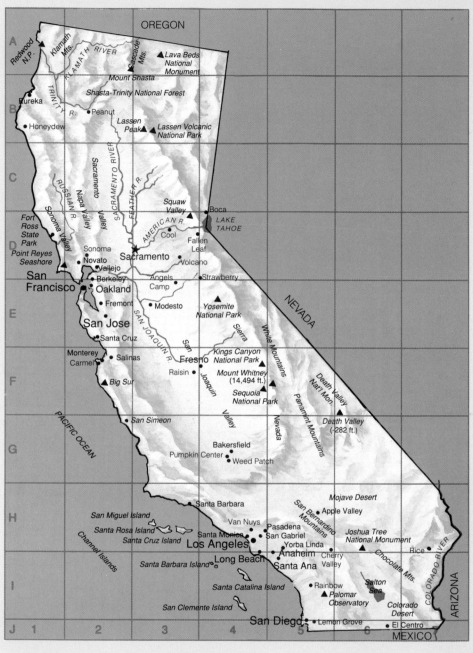

GLOSSARY

ancient: Relating to a time early in history

aqueduct: A canal made by people for sending water from one place to another

astronaut: A person who is highly trained for spaceflight

billion: A thousand million (1,000,000,000)

capital: The city that is the seat of government

capitol: The building where the government meets

climate: The typical weather of a region

coast: The land along a large body of water

county: The largest government division in a state; it has elected officials

desert: An area that receives little rainfall

dinosaurs: Huge animals that died out millions of years ago

drought: A period when rainfall is well below normal

explorer: A person who visits and studies unknown lands

forty-niner: A person who came to California during the 1849 gold rush

fossil: The remains of an animal or a plant that lived long ago and that have turned into rock

industry: A kind of business that has many workers to make products

interior: Inside; an inland area away from a seacoast

lava: Hot, melted rock that comes out of a volcano

mammoths and mastodons: Prehistoric animals that were much like today's elephants

manufacturing: The making of products

migrant farm worker: A worker who moves from farm to farm harvesting crops

million: A thousand thousand (1,000,000)

mission: A settlement around a Spanish Catholic church begun for the purpose of Christianizing Native Americans

population: The number of people in a place

presidio: A Spanish fort

pueblo: A Spanish town

reservation (Native American): Land in the United States that is set aside for Native Americans

sandal: A kind of shoe that is held together by straps

telescope: An instrument that makes distant objects look closer

union: A group that works for the rights of workers

universe: All of space and everything that is in it

volcano: A mountain from which lava and other materials erupt

wildlife refuge: Places where animals are protected

yucca: A kind of shrub or tree that grows in the Southwest, including the Joshua tree

INDEX

Page numbers in boldface type indicate illustrations.

ABOUT THE AUTHOR

Dennis Brindell Fradin is the author of 150 published children's books. His works for Childrens Press include the Young People's Stories of Our States series, the Disaster! series, and the Thirteen Colonies series. Dennis is married to Judith Bloom Fradin, who taught high-school and college English for many years. She is now Dennis's chief researcher. The Fradins are the parents of two sons, Anthony and Michael, and a daughter, Diana. Dennis graduated from Northwestern University in 1967 with a B.A. in creative writing, and has lived in Evanston, Illinois, since that year.